Alphabet Ice Cream

Sue Heap and Nick Sharratt

PUFFIN

Aa

a is for apple

b is for bat

B b

Cc

c is for crocodile, camel and cat

d is for digger

Dd

E e egg starts with e

g is for grasshopper

h is for honey

Hh

Ii

i is for ice cream to eat when it's sunny

k is for kite **Kk**

m is for
monkey

M m

Nick starts with n

Nn

Oo

o is for octopus

p is for pen

P p

rose starts with r **Rr**

Quack!

Ss

s is for Sue and spaghetti and star

track, train and tortoise all start with t

U u u is for unicorn

X x

x can mean
kiss

and yum and yuk too

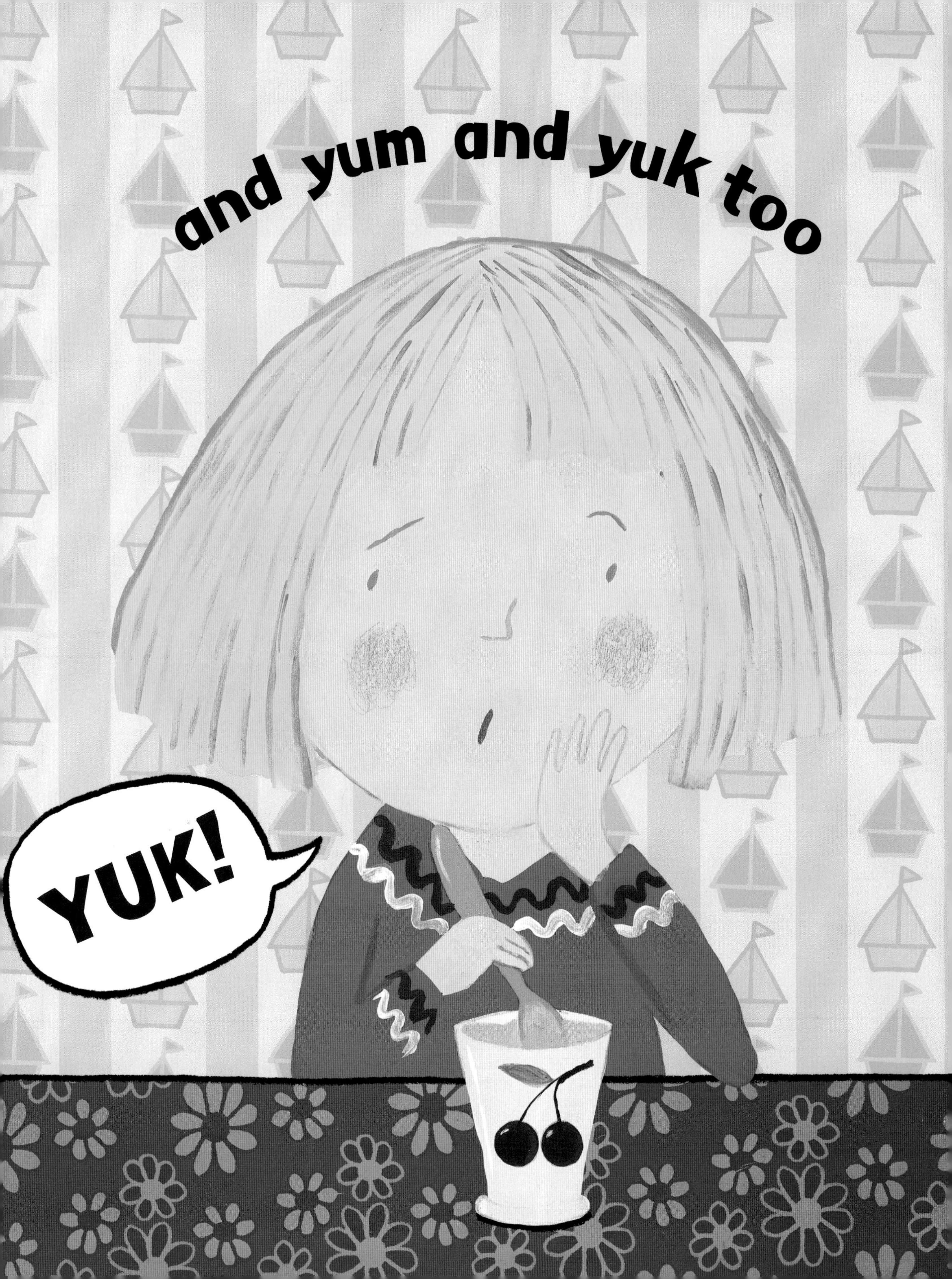

Zz

z is for...

ZOOM

Goodbye Nick and Sue!

PUFFIN BOOKS

Published by the Penguin Group: London, New York,
Australia, Canada, India, Ireland, New Zealand and South Africa
Penguin Books Ltd, Registered Offices:
One Embassy Gardens, 8 Viaduct Gardens, London SW11 7BW

puffinbooks.com

First published 2006
Published in this edition 2007
019
Copyright © Sue Heap and Nick Sharratt, 2006
All rights reserved
The moral right of the author and illustrator has been asserted
Manufactured in China
ISBN: 978–0–141–50062–1